ROBERT GIBBINGS

Uniform with this volume
THOMAS BEWICK
by Graham Reynolds

THE WOOD-ENGRAVINGS

OF

ROBERT GIBBINGS

BY THOMAS BALSTON

LONDON : ART AND TECHNICS : 1949

First published December 1949, *reprinted February* 1950 *by*
ART AND TECHNICS LTD 58 FRITH STREET LONDON WI
and printed in Great Britain by
THE SHENVAL PRESS LTD LONDON AND HERTFORD

CONTENTS

ILLUSTRATIONS

BOOKS ILLUSTRATED BY ROBERT GIBBINGS

A. Published by the Golden Cockerel Press

The Golden Cockerel Press's Spring Announcements 1930 *included a sample page of* Paradise Lost *decorated by Gibbings, but the volume was published in* 1936 *with engravings by Mary Groom.*

B. Published by Other Publishers

★

We are grateful to the following publishers who have kindly lent
electros of engravings for this book: Constable and Co., J. M. Dent and
Son, Golden Cockerel Press, Hodder and Stoughton, John Lane, The
Bodley Head; and to Jonathan Cape, Gerald Duckworth and Co., Faber
and Faber, William Heinemann, the Limited Editions Club of New
York, Methuen and Co., and the Orient Line Company for permission
to reproduce. Details of books from which engravings have been taken
will be found in the foregoing list.

From *Mr Glasspoole and the Chinese Pirates* 1935

went and drew a castle near Kinsale Harbour. A year later, at boarding school, he found a boy who copied prints with pen and ink, and this inspired him to do the same. These early efforts pleased his parents, but when, at the age of fourteen or fifteen he announced his desire to become an artist, he met with the firmest veto from his father on the grounds (1) that he would starve and (2) that he would have to look at naked women. So at eighteen he was sent to University College to become a doctor. In his first year he passed the First Arts Examination, but during the next two years he failed three times to pass the First Medical, partly through a sensitiveness which gave him an invincible horror of the wards (though he felt none of the usual qualms in the dissecting room), but chiefly because his heart was elsewhere. Then his father recognized the inevitable, but there was only money enough to pay for tuition under a local land-scape-painter, Harry Scully, RHA, from whom he had already taken some lessons during his university course. So he spent a year at home, drawing and painting with all his energy, but with little or no encouragement from his family or neighbours, and it was not till October 1911, when he was twenty-two, that he was able to get to London with enough money to keep him at the Slade School for a term. There Professor Brown consented to his starting in the Life Class instead of the Antique Room because he would be staying so short a time. Among his companions in the Life Class were Stanley Spencer, C. R. W. Nevinson, Mark Gertler and William Roberts, and he remembers how little they all thought of his abilities until Spencer happened to see one of his drawings of a cow.

In December he returned to Cork, but by April of the next year, 1912, he had secured money enough to see him through four more terms, and from then till Midsummer 1913 he worked three days a week at the Slade. But, what was far more important to his career, he also attended two days and some evenings at the Central School to study book illustration under Noel Rooke, the pioneer of 'modern' wood-engraving in England, and there he received his first instruction in design. It was a talk with Rooke that finally settled his career:

'Is it very foolish of me,' he asked in a moment of desperation, 'to try to be an artist?'

'What else could you do?'

'Nothing.'

'Isn't that the answer?' Rooke said kindly, being convinced that Gibbings had an aptitude for art.

When Gibbings reached the Central School, it was eight years since Rooke, dissatisfied with the mechanical reproduction of drawings which had dominated book illustration since the middle 'eighties, had turned his attention to the woodblock. Already for some years Ricketts and Shannon and Lucien Pissarro had been demonstrating that the same man should be both designer and engraver, but even so it seemed to Rooke that they were not using the woodblock and graver rightfully as an independent medium but only as a means of making copies of pen or pencil drawings. His idea was that wood-engravings should be designed by the artist, graver in hand, as engravings *per se* and not as engravings of drawings.[1]

During the next few years Rooke made engravings himself, and also aroused the interest of Eric Gill, who had been his fellow-student under Edward Johnston. But until 1915 Gill only engraved letters designed by Johnston or himself and a few small devices, bookplates and Christmas cards, and these, like Rooke's engravings

[1] It is interesting to note, as showing how obscure are the beginnings of any modern movement in art, that neither Pissarro, a Frenchman who had only been in England about ten years, nor Rooke, who had passed much of his life in French circles in France, was aware then, and for some years after, of the contemporary development of the 'modern' woodcut in France which was to achieve such publicity and popularity during the First World War.

and the many excellent designs which Gwendolen Raverat executed from 1909 onwards, were seen by very few people. In 1912, when Gibbings joined Rooke's class, Rooke seems to have recognized that he had now a pupil who might advance the art, and by the time Gibbings left the class in 1913 he had engraved three blocks for a colour print to illustrate a printed broadside of a poem of his own. Back at home he made a drawing of a cow which struck him as more suitable for a wood-engraving, and soon afterwards designed and engraved *The Pilot Boat*. It has proved impossible to find a print of this block, but it is remembered by those who saw it as giving the first indications of the special quality which afterwards distinguished his *Dublin under Snow* and Macedonian designs. In the next twelve months he executed a few more small engravings, all the time appearing to his family and neighbours as a confirmed loafer. And then came August 4th, 1914.

On that date, at 10 a.m., Gibbings, now twenty-five, presented himself at the Orderly Room of the 4th Royal Munster Fusiliers. Eleven days later he was given a commission in that battalion, and soon after joined a course of instruction for forty young officers. His father was surprised and pleased to get a private report that he was the most efficient of his class. Since then no one has ever complained that he is a loafer.

In 1915 he was posted to the 1st Battalion of his regiment, then in Gallipoli, and it was in action with them that he was shot through the throat on June 28th. After many months in hospitals, he returned home on sick leave in 1916, and there was inspired by a photograph to design *Retreat from Serbia* which he engraved on two blocks, and printed in flat colours on a letter-copying press.[1] By the autumn he was again fit for duty, and stationed in the Royal Barracks, Dublin; and it was from a window of the mess-room there that he made

[1] The copies in the Printrooms of the British Museum and the Victoria and Albert were printed later with graduated colours on each block.

the drawing for his first important engraving, *Dublin under Snow*. In January 1917 he was sent to Salonica, where he designed *City Walls, Salonica* and *A Street in Macedonia* in the six weeks before he was invalided to Malta. There he drew the magnificent *tondo, Melleha*, the big oblong *Hamrun* and some smaller works. But after four months he was returned to England in the ill-fated Llandovery Castle, of which he afterwards made a three-colour engraving. Back in London he was posted to the Ministry of Munitions, resumed his attendance at Rooke's evening class, and settled in the Bolton Studios, Redcliffe Road, a district to which he has remained faithful on all his later sojourns in London. There he proceeded to engrave some of his wartime designs and, with Rooke's approbation, bought himself a Crown Albion Press. Six months later, in March 1918, he was invalided out of the Army and started his career as an independent artist on a handsome gratuity, most of which, however, he lost by investing in a French loan. But otherwise the fates were kind. He very soon achieved a considerable reputation as an engraver and, for two years, enjoyed prosperity.

Slowly and surely during the war years the 'modern' woodcut had been creeping into notice. In 1914 and 1915 Wyndham Lewis' *Blast* had appeared with some cubistic prints: in 1915 the Hampshire House Workshops had published Eric Gill's *Devil's Devices*, and the Poetry Bookshop Frances Cornford's *Spring Morning* with wood-cuts by Gwendolen Raverat, the first English books illustrated with 'modern' engravings: and others, most of them by foreign artists, appeared in Austin Spare's magazine, *Form* (1917). By 1918 there were many artists in London interesting themselves in wood, but some of them had ideals and methods very different from those of the modernists, one set, for instance, following the practice of Morley Fletcher and J. D. Batten and making side-grain cuts in the Japanese manner which they printed with paste and water, another generally engraving but sometimes cutting in the old European manner and printing with printers' (varnish) ink. And among the modernists themselves there was at first a strong bias in favour of the coloured print, fostered by Malcolm Salaman in the *Studio*, where he sedulously preached that 'the wood-block colour-print is likely to become an important element of house decoration', i.e. in the myriads of small houses being built after the war. In this welter of ideas it was difficult for a young artist to find his right path, and Gibbings at first spent much of his energy on the colour-print. But, though his designs were not lacking in strength, the printers' varnish ink with which they were printed, being only semi-transparent, devitalized the colouring, especially where one colour was super-imposed upon another. But they had one good effect, in that they so much interested Salaman that he published a long article on Gibbings' work in the *Studio* of January 1919, and so introduced it to a large public. The article was illustrated with two colour-prints, *The Retreat from Serbia* and *Evening at Gaza*, two reproductions of colour-prints in black and white, and four reproductions of black and white engravings. 'Now that the war is over,' the text ended, 'Captain Gibbings, wisely recognizing the universal call for bright-ness and charm, is engaged upon some delightful schemes for colour-prints with the pictorial graces of childhood and girlhood decoratively appealing.' Gibbings, however, was not so engaged, and, anyhow, he was so dissatisfied with his next colour-print, *Albert Bridge, Chelsea*, which appeared in *Modern Woodcuts and Lithographs*, the *Studio* year-book for 1919, that he turned to more ambitious black and white engravings than he had previously attempted, *Melleha* and *Hamrun* based on his Mediterranean draw-ings, and *Clear Waters* (pages 42 to 44).

With these three large blocks Gibbings definitely established him-self among the leaders of the movement, and it was he who suggested to Rooke and Sydney Lee that they should found a society to further their aims. Many engravers of all sorts were consulted, and eventually Mrs Austen Brown, whose husband was a colour-engraver in the Japanese style, summoned them to a meeting at which it was proposed to found a society with Pissarro, Lee and Rooke at its head. But it soon became clear that a single society could not adequately represent so many divergent ideas. After further meetings in Gibbings' studio (by then at 35 Redcliffe Square) and finally at Philip Hagreen's, from which the Japanese party abstained, it was decided to form the Society of Wood Engravers with Gibbings as its Honorary Secretary. There were ten original members, Pissarro, Lee and Gordon Craig of the older school, and Rooke, Gibbings, Gill, Gwen Raverat, Hagreen, John Nash and Dickey with more definitely 'modern' aims.

In November 1920 the new Society held its first Annual Exhibition at the Chenil Gallery in King's Road, with a catalogue introduced by Campbell Dodgson of the British Museum, a warm supporter from the start. Of the ninety engravings shown seventy-nine were by members, and the rest by Ethelbert White, Rupert Lee, E. F. Daglish, Desmond Chute, Ludovic Rodo, Dorothy M. Elliot and Margaret Pilkington. Gibbings was the largest contributor with twelve prints, of which all but one, a little *Corner in Malta*, were black and white.

The exhibition aroused much interest, but even before it opened some big commercial firms had noted the new engraving's potentialities for advertisements, and were paying high prices. Gibbings' first commission of this kind was for seven blocks with eastern subjects to advertise the Matinée Cigarettes of the Imperial Tobacco Company, and he was very soon inundated with a host of similar commissions and proposals for many more. In these halcyon days he caused the Baynard Press to print 125 copies of *Twelve Wood Engravings*, a selection from his early works, which he published himself, and then, in the summer of 1921, retired to Cornwall to work on his commissions without interruption. But suddenly a slump set in, all the proposals were withdrawn, and even some of the definite commissions were cancelled. By this time he had greatly increased his responsibilities, and by the end of the year he was finding it hard to make both ends meet.

The next two years were a struggle. Though he had eight exhibits in the Society's second show (November 1921), five in the third (1922) and six in the fourth (1923), the sales of independent engravings were not nearly enough to support him. He managed, however, to secure various small commissions, including some for book-jackets, and he began to teach wood-engraving. But it was a restless hand-to-mouth existence until Jonathan Cape engaged him to do thirty-eight headpieces and tailpieces for a new edition of *Erewhon* (1923), the first of his many illustrated books, and Harold Taylor, the founder of the Golden Cockerel Press, commissioned ten blocks for Brantôme's *Lives of Gallant Ladies* (1924).

This introduction to the Golden Cockerel proved one of the luckiest incidents in Gibbings' career, for while he was working on the Brantôme blocks, for which he was to receive £100, he suddenly learnt that Taylor's health had given way and that the Press was to be dismantled. With the financial support of a friend and characteristic energy, he intervened just in time to prevent the dispersal of the plant and workmen, and bought the Press lock, stock and barrel.

The instruction which Gibbings had received in Rooke's class had all been in definite relation to letterpress, but since leaving it he had only designed independent prints. He had not, however, lost all interest in work with type: as early as 1922 he had written, 'I should very much like to do some decorations for really first-class books, especially where it would be possible to keep in touch with the printer and treat the book as a whole.' Now, in January 1924, he found himself in a position where all his engraving would be in

From *Count Stefan* 1928

relation to type, and with the advantage that he could choose what texts he would decorate and control every detail of the book's design and manufacture. And he was lucky to have reached this position, so perfectly suited to his abilities, at a moment when there started a boom of Private Press books which was to last for seven years.

In its three years under Taylor the Press had published seventeen books, of which only one contained wood-engravings. From the first Gibbings was intent on the decorated book, and of the seventy-two published in his nine years of control forty-eight were adorned with wood-engravings and ten with copper engravings. The remaining fourteen were straightforward reprints, undertaken because he found that planning four or five decorated books a year absorbed all his energies, whereas it required at least eight books to keep his staff in full employment. Among the fourteen wood-engravers whom he employed, many of them on their first books, were John Nash, David Jones, Eric Ravilious, Blair Hughes-Stanton, John Farleigh and Agnes Miller-Parker, all now of established reputation, but the bulk of the work was done by himself with nineteen volumes to his name (he illustrated another six after he had relinquished control of the Press) and by Eric Gill with fifteen. In the first fifteen months Gill's work was limited to *Sonnets and Verses* by his sister, Enid Clay, and some initial letters which were first employed in Browning's *Pictor Ignotus*, but later, at his own suggestion, he was paid a small retaining fee in return for which he engraved exclusively for the Press, except a few small items which he placed elsewhere with Gibbings' consent. So began the close collaboration between Gibbings as planner and typographer and Gill as decorator which produced the Press's best-known masterpieces, *The Canterbury Tales* (1929–31) and, even more important, *The Four Gospels* (1931).

Success was not, of course, immediate. Only once, many years earlier, when he was attending the Central School, had Gibbings set up type, composing, under J. H. Mason's eye, his own one poem in several sizes of type with various leading. In 1924 he had still nearly everything to learn about type, paper, ink and presswork, and absolutely everything about the administration of a press and the marketing of books. But he was lucky that the type he took over was several sizes of Caslon Old Face, and he continued to employ founts of this on all his books until seven years later, when he acquired the Golden Cockerel Face, designed for him by Gill and cut by Messrs W. H. Caslon, and used it on *The Four Gospels* and a few later books. He was less lucky in starting with a stock of Arnold paper, which was far too hard and white for the 18 pt. type and very black engravings of his first decorated book, Henry Carey's *Songs and Poems*. But thereafter he generally employed more harmonious papers, especially Batchelor's handmade. Perhaps the first volume in which the type, paper and decorations made a pleasing whole was the *Sonnets and Verses*, which was crowned by the Double Crown Club as the best-printed book of the year.[1]

[1] It must be admitted that this award, voted by a majority of the members, so much dissatisfied some eminent typographers of the Club that it very nearly led to the Club's disruption.

When Gibbings took over the Press at Waltham St Lawrence, he was delighted to be established in the country. 'I think,' he wrote, 'it is going to be very jolly. There is a pleasant cottage with three-quarters of an acre of garden, and with any luck I should have quite a lot of spare time for my own work.' But eight months later he had learnt that being the controller and typographer and often the illustrator of a press was no half-time job. 'It's surprising,' he then wrote, 'how easy it is to make our books go, but I'm tied by the leg as I watch everything, and every sheet is passed before going through the press. It's hard work when I'm illustrating three books. I see no chance of a holiday for myself, much as I'd like one.' After two years, however, he had got the work so well organized that he could get abroad for a month or two in the summer, and even undertake a few small blocks for other publishers. But all this employment with his own and other artists' woodblocks temporarily sickened him of wood: he began to hanker after paint, but he found it impossible to combine painting and engraving in a working week, and only succeeded in painting a few pictures on his holidays. 'I'd willingly,' he wrote at this time, 'consign all wood to the flames in favour of the oil.'

In 1929 this tension was relieved by a longer and eventful break. Among the outside commissions he had accepted was one from Houghton Mifflin of New York for twelve engravings to Esther Forbes' *A Mirror for Witches*, and in forwarding the invoice for his blocks he added, just to give a friendly personal note to his letter, 'Next time you give me a job, for God's sake send me to the South Seas. I'm sick of English fogs.' To his surprise Houghton Mifflin replied immediately that they were delighted with the idea, and that one of their directors would soon be in London to discuss it. The result was a commission to sail to Tahiti, a place he had long wanted to visit, in January 1929, to get into contact there with James Norman Hall, and arrange with him about doing a book together.

He made the contact, and they agreed upon a scheme. But Gibbings could stay only four months in Tahiti, and Hall, who was deep in work for an American edition of *The Mutiny of the Bounty*, could spare little time for writing. When the time was up, Gibbings had made many drawings, but there was still no manuscript. Arrived home, he engraved many of the drawings, hoping that they would somehow fit Hall's text whenever he wrote it. But after two years Hall begged Houghton Mifflin to let him off, as he was busy on further volumes of the Bounty series. Houghton Mifflin then asked Gibbings to suggest a suitable text for his engravings, but he could think of none, and finally in despair suggested that with the aid of notes and letters he had written in Tahiti, he should compile a largely imaginary account of his adventures, which they could accept or not when they saw it. So *Iorana* was composed, and Gibbings was started on his new career of author and illustrator combined. His previous published writings were limited to *The Seventh Man, a true Cannibal Tale of the South Sea Islands, told in fifteen Wood-Engravings and precisely one hundred and eighty-nine words* (Golden Cockerel Press, 1930), and a short article on the Press in Herbert Furst's annual *The Woodcut* (1927).

Though the Press was now so well organized, the inevitable result of its controller's absence appeared the following year (1930) when its output, which was normally nine or ten volumes, sank to six, of which two were very slight. It remained at this lower level in 1931, but that may have been due to the exceptional labour involved in the planning and production of *The Four Gospels*. In 1932 the number of publications rose to twelve, of which the largest and most original was Eric Ravilious' *Twelfth Night*, and the Press also printed the small folio *Fourteen Wood Engravings by Robert Gibbings* for the Orient Line, very vigorous designs from drawings he had made on cruises.

Meanwhile, in September 1931, England had gone off gold, the

Publisher's device

value of the pound had fallen by about a third, and everyone, almost enthusiastically, had taken to economizing. Among the first victims was the book-trade. A large proportion of the standing orders which had for some years absorbed practically the whole output of the Press were cancelled, and many copies of the 1932 books were left on its hands. Their prices, which had been arranged with an apparent certainty of selling the whole editions immediately, were too low for the new conditions, and the value of the business, into which Gibbings had ploughed back all the profits of the seven good years (the Golden Cockerel Face type alone had cost him more than £1,000), slumped badly. Even before the slump, when the business seemed, in Gibbings' words, '100 per cent better than it has ever been before, with all the books sold out for the next twelve months,' he had felt 'tempted to sell the blooming bird' because he was 'simply hunted to death with work' which interfered with his growing desire to paint. By the spring of 1933 he found it financially impossible to keep the Press going, and in August of that year he sold it for what it would fetch.

For some months Gibbings remained at Waltham in a one-room hut which he had built in the orchard, living on a few commissions. Early in 1934 Constable engaged him to illustrate Helen Waddell's *Beasts and Saints*, and he retired to Cornwall for a year while he was completing the work. Then he returned to Waltham, and early in 1936 was appointed Lecturer in Book Production at Reading University. His duties occupied three days a week (and often an uncovenanted fourth) during the three University terms, and it was agreed that his subject should be wood-engraving in connection with typography. He found that he enjoyed both the teaching and the company of many well-informed colleagues, and continued to hold the post for seven years, employing his spare time in illustrating many books, of which the most important was a three-volume *Morte d'Arthur* for the Limited Editions Club of New York, and taking advantage of the vacations for extensive travel. One Long Vacation he went to Bermuda, and the following spring to the Red Sea, and so obtained the material for his Penguin book *Blue Angels and Whales* (1938), which introduced him to a large public, and thrilled it with his descriptions of underwater life, illustrated by sketches actually drawn on xylonite twenty feet below sea level.

In the summer of 1939 the state of international affairs forbad any distant travel, and he started exploring the Thames from its source to the sea, 'a neat and compact little journey' he calls it, in a flat-bottomed boat of his own design built in the University's woodwork department. But he had only got as far down the river as Mapledurham when the war broke out. He offered to do camouflage or to make drawings from submarines, but the staffs of universities were asked to remain at their posts; and anyhow the effects of his old wound unfitted him for active service. So at intervals during the autumn and winter, partly on patrol in the naval Home Guard, he continued his exploration of the river, and in the summer of the next year had completed the text and fifty woodblocks of *Sweet Thames\Run Softly*, which both here and in America had instant success. In England alone, in spite of paper restrictions, it went through ten large editions in seven years.

Encouraged by this success he spent his free time of the next eighteen months exploring the Wye, mostly from a cottage which he acquired on its upper reaches, where he could indulge to the full his passion for solitary observation varied by occasional excursions among his country neighbours: and the result was *Coming Down the Wye* (1942). Then, feeling that five months' vacation a year was insufficient for work of this kind, he resigned his lectureship and in January 1943 retired for an idyllic fifteen months to south-west Ireland where he wrote his happy, rambling *Lovely is the Lee* (1944).

It is not difficult to see why, with these three River Books, Gibbings became one of the most popular authors of the English-speaking world. Their texts, illuminated by the many apposite engravings, are an entrancing hotch-potch of descriptions of scenery, anecdotes, dialogues, folk-lore, vivid observations of birds, beasts, fishes and human beings by a very keen-eyed and well-read naturalist, and even, though he consigns all guide-books to the devil, historical facts culled from a wide range of reading. And all this information is given in paragraph after paragraph which flows as smoothly as the rivers in their lower reaches. Sometimes, as in the early chapters on the Thames book, where he is gliding down the river in his boat, one would say that the water had entered into his soul, and elsewhere, as in the Wye book, where he surveyed the river more from the banks, walking or driving, the pace of the written word increases, and produces such perfect sequences as his description of the river's source:

'I was at the source of the Wye. After a gentle murmuring underground the water welled up, brushing aside the young spring grass, to form a pool no bigger than a bowler hat. Then gently it glided between the rich tussocks of moss and rushes still bent from their load of winter snow, until it tumbled like a shower of sequins over the black velvet of the peat face. The pool below this was wider and deeper, and with every yard of its flow the strength of the rivulet increased. Small streams from successive dells and dingles joined in, and so, between thick felts of spagnum moss starred with cotton grass, and over rocks long since worn smooth, it frisked and dived towards its first main tributary a thousand feet below.' It was of such writing that Hugh Walpole said 'Gibbings writes as he breathes, so naturally (he is a vast-chested man) that it scarcely seems to be written at all'.

Lovely is the Lee was Gibbings' tribute to the land and people most dear to him, and on VJ Day 1945, when travel was again permitted, he sailed for his other love, the South Sea islands, and only returned to England in November 1947, after spending six months in New Zealand and eighteen in Polynesia. For long periods he lived with the natives of the islands, and became a high chief of one of them. His latest book, *Over the Reefs* (1948), on which he has worked for more than three years, is an intimate, lively and often unique account of episodes in their daily life, abundantly illustrated with engravings of scenes and objects which have never been depicted before.

Now, in his sixtieth year, at an age when eye-strain has compelled most engravers to desist, he is planning to 'lose himself once again among the hills and valleys of Ireland, where he belongs', not, of course, without the determination to produce a book even nearer to his standard of perfection.

THERE are well over one thousand engravings by Gibbings in published books, another hundred perhaps have appeared as independent prints, and he has engraved a host of blocks for commercial advertising. The examples of his work here reproduced, as far as possible in chronological order, have been selected to show both his technical progress from his early blocks to the consummate mastery of his illustrations in *Over the Reefs* (1948), and also the changes of his artistic vision from the broad pattern-making of his first distinguished work to the almost Bewickian naturalism of his latest.

His first designs were very simple, but they are interesting partly because of the originality at that date of such massing of black and white, and partly as instances of Gibbings' instinct to accommodate his designs to his technical resources, which were then only those of a beginner. But, though during three war years he had had little or no opportunity of improving his technique, *Dublin under Snow* (1917) has a genuine aesthetic value. In it he has succeeded in imposing an almost cubistic design upon a fundamentally impressionist conception without sacrificing atmosphere or texture. It is remarkable that he had then had no opportunity of seeing cubistic work. This was followed by *City Walls of Salonica*, *Melleha* and *Hamrun*, all three designed in 1917 and engraved in 1918, in which the sight of the cubic houses of the Eastern Mediterranean in the strong southern sunlight has imposed even more cubistic patterns on designs which with all their simplification are still naturalistic or impressionist, rendering all lighted surfaces in solid white, and all shadow in solid black.

There is one interesting technical device in these engravings which Gibbings discovered for himself. In *Dublin under Snow*, wherever one white plane is partly in front of another, he has omitted the normal bounding line of the front plane, and left it to the spectator's imagination to complete its shape and so separate the planes. In *City Walls* he has used the same device with his black planes, but separated the white with thin black lines. In *Melleha* he reverted to separating only the black planes, but in *Hamrun*, for the first time, neither black nor white are separated.

For some years Gibbings frequently employed this device, and with increasing boldness. In the earlier prints the 'vanished' lines were all straight, and less than half an inch long, but in *Hamrun* one of them extends to nearly an inch and a half, and in *Clear Waters*, his *tour-de-force* in this style, the curved upper outlines of the girl's arms are left entirely to the spectator's imagination, so cleverly that he is hardly aware that they are not indicated on the paper. The effect, especially in *Hamrun* and *Clear Waters* where the backgrounds are white, is an almost dazzling luminosity.[1]

In these first years after the war Gibbings made many other independent prints, nearly all of them characterized by his unfailingly effective balance of black and white masses. At first many of these blocks were small, but he gradually concentrated on the larger sizes where his strong patterning had greater scope. But in 1923 he was recalled to smaller work by his first commission to decorate a book, Cape's edition of *Erewhon*. For most of these small headpieces and tailpieces he for the first time employed the black silhouette,

[1] Though Gibbings certainly invented the 'vanished' line for himself, it had been previously employed by Edward Wadsworth in at least two prints which, owing to his absence in Ireland and the Eastern Mediterranean, Gibbings had had no opportunity of seeing. The first was a cubist print of 1914, *A Yorkshire Village*, and the second *Rotterdam* which appeared in Wyndham Lewis' *Blast* (vol. II, 1915). Wadsworth again employed the device in his designs of camouflaged ships in dry dock (1918).

From *Erewhon* 1923

generally relieved by a few thin white lines, and it was in the practice of this new style that he first had the pleasurable sensation of engraving with the firmness and cleanness at which he aimed, especially in the *Top hat* (above). This was a static subject, but he continued to experiment with the silhouette until he could render textures and movement with the grace and subtlety of the *Leopard* (page 63) in Driberg's *Initiation* (1932).

This introduction to bookwork proved, as we have seen, one of the turning points of his career. He had early recognized that the emotions aroused in him by almost every manifestation of beauty (colour, he has stated, is what first attracts him to a subject) were so strong as to require a strait-jacket, and he had taken to wood-engraving because 'the technique is austere, and there are no happy accidents'. He now learnt that engraving for books entailed an even stricter discipline than independent work. 'Type,' he wrote, 'has taken centuries to reach its present form, and its chief fault is its almost too perfect finish. If engravings are to harmonize with type, they must in some way approximate to its finish.' And so from that date nine-tenths of his efforts have been concentrated on books. He set himself to tackle the problem posed by the Royal Society of Arts in 1776, when they offered the prize for 'the best engraving on wood for illustrating works in art or science or for decorating books, and capable of being worked off with the letterpress'.

From the moment that he began to engrave for books, Gibbings had found it essential to modify his style: the black and white masses of his independent engravings could not possibly be wedded to type. Nor would any one style of engraving be suitable for all the books, of very various sizes and lay-outs, which he must design for the Press if it was to retain the public's interest. He was therefore driven partly to employ other artists, but often to adapt his own engraving to different lay-outs, and so acquired a versatility which he might otherwise have missed. This was further necessitated by the very varied subject matter of the books which ranged from Lucian to Flaubert among foreign writers and from Swift to Lord Grey among the English.

In the years from 1923 to 1939 Gibbings made engravings for forty-seven books, of which twenty-seven were printed by the Golden Cockerel Press and twenty by other printers. Most of the engravings in the latter class were either small silhouettes or small vignettes, and some of the smaller Press books were similarly decorated. But at least a dozen of the Press books contained larger and more strongly patterned designs, some within rectangular frames and some vignettes, which would have overpowered the light modern types of the normal publishers' books, but could be balanced by the Press's Caslon Old Face. Perfect balance, of course, was not achieved all at once: the engravings to *Samson and Delilah*, though their black and white masses are already relieved by greyer passages which did not occur in the independent engravings, still remain too strong for letterpress. But gradually these masses were eliminated, the designs became more linear and more complex until, by 1935 at the latest, perfect balance was achieved in *The Wreck of the Whale-Ship Essex* which, incidentally, he also edited. Considered apart from their settings in books, these engravings are remarkable for their strength and balance and the originality of their designs. On a smaller scale, but with much of their monumental quality, are the two series of small square blocks which, with the aid of very few

From *Over the Reefs* 1948

words, tell Gibbings' own stories, *The Seventh Man* (pages 55 and 56) and *A True Tale of Love in Tonga* (pages 77–80).

In nearly all his bookwork from 1923 to 1936 Gibbings was rather a decorator than an illustrator, but from 1936 onwards there has been a change of aim. We have seen how almost accidentally he came to write *Iorana* (1932), but this started him on the path of authorship. *Coconut Island* (1936), a children's story of adventures in the South Seas, was clearly inspired by an impulse to write, and the engravings in it, though their decorative function is never overlooked, were primarily designed to elucidate the text where words alone would have proved inadequate. The same is true of *Blue Angels and Whales* (1938), the three River Books (1940–44) and *Over the Reefs* (1948). He has, in fact, become an illustrator in the fullest sense, but this is to cast no aspersion on the engravings, which, partly because he could now afford to spend more time on them, become progressively finer in point of execution and certainly not inferior in design. The last four of these books, excellently printed under his own supervision by the Temple Press, Letchworth, are all remarkable for their well-balanced pages, and in the lighter and more detailed engravings of *Over the Reefs*, on which the success of the River Books enabled

C

him to spend three years, he has achieved his finest harmonies with modern letterpress.

Though working to his own texts was the occasion of this final development of the representational element in Gibbings' work, it cannot be considered as in any way fortuitous. We have seen that his early engravings, though they were hailed by such a judge as Dr Campbell Dodgson in his Introduction to *Contemporary English Woodcuts* (1922) as Cubist or Post-Impressionist, were fundamentally representational: and there is a general trend throughout his work from his black masses to more detailed surfaces, *pari passu* with his increasing technical skill. There were some setbacks, due either to the nature of the type or text with which he was working, or to the necessity of completing his work more quickly than detailed representation would allow. 'In the old days,' he writes, 'I had to make the time I spent on a job fit the price I was getting for it.' But the goal was never in doubt. The deepest source of his inspiration, expressed in his contribution to *Sermons by Artists* (Golden Cockerel Press, 1934), is the mystical belief that 'out of the riot of forms and colours in nature the artificer is able to co-ordinate the elements of a more comprehensible design', and so 'for brief moments reaches harmony with the universal spirit. Sometimes in those seconds of insight time stands still, events past, present and future remain stationary like resting cattle spotted on the surface of a field, and the artist sees them as God sees time'. To such an outlook natural objects and the designing mind are equally essential to the Beatific Vision.

Gibbings' passionate observation of scenes and objects of every kind, helped and inspired by an unusual keenness of vision, might have landed him in almost photographic realism if it had been under less intellectual control. As a countryman, a craftsman and a naturalist he started his art career with a wide repertory of subjects, and this has been continually increased by travel and other experience. It makes no difference whether he is portraying birds, beasts or fishes, buildings, boats or implements, trees or flowers, landscapes or sea-scapes, northern or tropical, they are all things seen and studied, and are all rendered with equal mastery. Nor has he neglected human beings. His complaint in *Sermons by Artists* that 'in texture of epidermis there are few creatures more repellent than a civilized human' was a joke, and it is for technical reasons, not for any lack of appreciation of the human form, that he has done comparatively little figure work. 'Wood engraving,' he has explained, 'is essentially white on black. For dark-skinned people it is a perfect medium, because with them it is a matter of engraving lights on dark. But for light-skinned people one needs dark accents on white, and you cannot engrave dark accents: you can only engrave round them, and I have always disliked the black line.' He has often, however, with much success employed the Polynesians, though they are lightly pigmented, as small moving details in land or seascapes, and he has engraved at least one striking portrait of a white man, which is said to be an excellent likeness (page 54). He has also caricatured white people with success in a few humorous designs.

A large repertory and great technical skill are good assets, but it is vision and sincerity which make the work of art. It is clear throughout Gibbings' work that he has an exact mental image of his design, and that every mark of the graver is there with a definite purpose. And, because he is a man of strong individuality, his designs have the individuality, the uniqueness, which is the prime essential. He was lucky perhaps that he started engraving when the 'modern' woodcut was in its infancy, and there was no risk of being distracted from his own personal vision by the works of previous masters. Anyhow, with very few exceptions (a few reminiscences of Eric Gill in one or two of the Golden Cockerel books), all his engravings, however much they differ among themselves in style and execution, are unmistakably his own.

THE ENGRAVINGS

1917 Dublin under Snow (reduced)

Scraps

Street in Macedonia

1921: from *Twelve Wood-Engravings*

Evening Sunshine

The Rickyard
1921: from *Twelve Wood-Engravings*

1918 Melleha, Malta (reduced)

1918 Hamrun (reduced)

1923 Hurdler: from *Erewhon*

1923 Horse and dogs: from *Erewhon*

OPPOSITE: Clear Waters (reduced)

1925 Samson and the Lion (reduced)
From *Samson and Delilah*

1925 Samson and the Philistines (reduced)
From *Samson and Delilah*

1925: from *Samson and Delilah* (reduced)

1926 Seascape: from *Fallodon Papers*

1933 Hare: from *Lord Adrian*

Fishing Boat

Haystacks

1927: from *The Charm of Birds*

Pochard Ducks

Mute Swans

1927: from *The Charm of Birds*

Fruit Seller

Card Party

1928: from *Swift's Poems*

1928 Snake: from *Lamia*

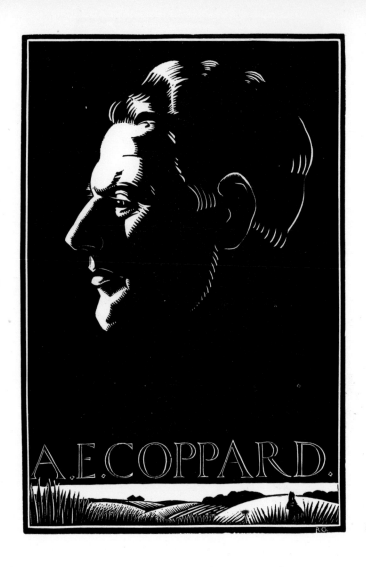

A.E.COPPARD.

1928 Portrait of the Author: from *Count Stefan*

1930 ABOVE: Captain O'Hara
BELOW: After suffering and hardship
From *The Seventh Man*

1930 ABOVE: Welcome from the Ladies
BELOW: 'Their grandson told me'
From *The Seventh Man*

1932: from *Crotty Shinkwin*

1932 Mediterranean Calm (reduced): from *XIV Engravings*

1932 Noontime in Italy (reduced): from *XIV Engravings*

1932 High Society, Grenada (reduced): from *XIV Engravings*

1932 Going to Market (reduced): from *XIV Engravings*

1932 ABOVE: Tahiti in Sight. BELOW: My House in Tahiti
From *Iorana*

1932 Crested Crane and Leopard: from *Initiation*

Trout

Perch

1933: from *The Roving Angler*

1934 Seagull (reduced): from *Glory of Life*

1934 Life and Death (reduced): from *Glory of Life*

1934 Snake in Forest (reduced): from *Glory of Life*

1934 Kingfishers (reduced): from *Glory of Life*

1934 Squirrel
From *Beasts and Saints*

1934 St Cuthbert's Birds
From *Beasts and Saints*

1934 Lion and Bear
From *Beasts and Saints*

1934 The Open Boat
From *The Voyage of the Bounty's Launch*

1934 The Open Boat at Sea
From *The Voyage of the Bounty's Launch*

1935 Boat Building (reduced)
From *The Journal of James Morrison*

1935 Harpooning
From *The Wreck of the Whale-Ship Essex*

Whale Leaping

Scouting for Whales

1935: from *The Wreck of the Whale-Ship Essex*

1935: from *A True Tale of Love in Tonga*

1935: from *A True Tale of Love in Tonga*

1935: from *A True Tale of Love in Tonga*

1935: from *A True Tale of Love in Tonga*

Pigs

Harvest

1936: from *The Twelve Months*

1936 Portrait of Fabre
From *The Insect Man*

Sheld Duck

Dabchick
1936: from *A Bird Diary*

1936 Tufted Duck: from *A Bird Diary*

OPPOSITE: 1936 Title-page (reduced)

LE MORTE DARTHUR

THE STORY OF KING ARTHUR & OF HIS
NOBLE KNIGHTS OF THE ROUND TABLE
WRITTEN BY SIR THOMAS MALORY,
FIRST PRINTED BY WILLIAM CAXTON,
NOW MODERNISED, AS TO SPELLING
AND PUNCTUATION, BY A. W. POLLARD,
ILLUSTRATED WITH WOOD ENGRAV-
INGS BY ROBERT GIBBINGS, & PRINTED
AT THE GOLDEN COCKEREL PRESS,
LONDON, FOR THE LIMITED EDITIONS
CLUB, NEW YORK, 1936
VOLUME I

Atoll (reduced)

1937 Cormorant
From *A Book of Uncommon Prayer*

Old Horse

Rat

1937: from *A Book of Uncommon Prayer*

Hulk

Convict Ship

1937: from *John Graham, Convict*

Kangaroos

Mrs Fraser's Escape

1937: from *John Graham, Convict*

Stage Coach

Pigs

1938: from *The Microbe Man*

Sleigh Picnic

Bicycle Picnic
1939: from *The Radium Woman*

1940 Frontispiece (reduced)
From *Othello*

Kingfisher

OPPOSITE: Widgeon

1940: from *Sweet Thames Run Softly*

Willows

Halfpenny Bridge, Lechlade

<small>OPPOSITE:</small> Fritillaries

1940: from *Sweet Thames Run Softly*

Floods, Clifton Hampden

Shillingford Bridge
1940: from *Sweet Thames Run Softly*

Glanrhyd

1942: from *Coming Down the Wye*

Tufted Duck

Cows

1942: from *Coming Down the Wye*

Illicit Trout

Glanrhyd under Snow

1942: from *Coming Down the Wye*

Sweat House

St Benen's Chapel

1944: from *Lovely is the Lee*

Ass and Cart

Connemara Cottage

Oyster Catchers

1944: from *Lovely is the Lee*

Old Boat

Carrigadrohid

Inniscarra

1944: from *Lovely is the Lee*

Gougane Barra

The Tan Bucket
1944: from *Lovely is the Lee*

1948 Papetoai Bay, Moorea:

from *Over the Reefs*

Pearl Diver's Basket

Ha'amonga (The Burden)

1948: from *Over the Reefs*

Fallen Pandanus

'The House that waited'
1948: from *Over the Reefs*

Pacific Sunset

The Village drum, Fangamalo
1948: from *Over the Reefs*

Native House, Mangaia

Tupé

Native Basket

1948: from *Over the Reefs*